Staying Safe While Sheltering in Place

Shari Schnuelle, LIMHP, LPC
&
Melissa Adams, LICSW, CDC
with Geri Henderson, Ph.D.

For information, contact
MSI Press
1760-F Airline Highway, #203
Hollister, CA 95023

Cover design & layout: Carl Leaver

Cover image: ShutterStock

Copyeditor: Mary Ann Raemisch

LCCN: pending

ISBN: 978-1-950328-43-7

Adams, Schnuelle, & Henderson

Contents

Adams, Schnuelle, & Henderson

Adams, Schnuelle, & Henderson

Staying Safe While Sheltering in Place

Adams, Schnuelle, & Henderson

Introduction

Geri Henderson, PhD

My eyes blinked open suddenly and I was immediately filled with dread, even terror! Now wide awake and worried, I envisioned a stay-at-home order being issued when I was a child. How would I have survived? I was immediately filled with fear as I imagined what it might have been like to be unable to escape the abuses of my father.

Of course, my next thought was for all the children, women, girlfriends, or anyone else who might now be stuck at home with a person who is dangerous, someone who instills fear in their victims day and night. What is happening to these children? What is happening to whole families who are in lock-down with someone who can, has, and probably will hurt them, possibly fatally?

I started talking to people, starting with my sisters. The thought of it was so awful they couldn't really discuss it, but one of them, who has worked for years in Social Services, told me that caseworkers and family support providers were helping children who had been removed connect with their parents remotely. I also heard an interview on NPR, National Public Radio, telling listeners that, for safety's sake, caseworkers were still going into homes, taking as many health precautions as they could. Since then, I have begun to hear about more outreach programs, because it's obvious that the need for family support during this time is critical.

The question that immediately follows must be, "How can severely abused spouses and children find the help they need?" Sometimes even making a phone call is dangerous. On one podcast, I heard that volunteers were staffing tables in supermarkets, bank lobbies (where available), and gas stations where people can get help as they run essential errands. That is not something that is widely available, however. The professionals contributing to this little volume have practical ideas of ways to be safe.

Boots pharmacies in the UK are offering safe spaces for domestic violence victims (BBC 5/01/2020). The BBC also reports that there has been a surge in violence since the lockdown began. Calls to the National Domestic Abuse hotline rose by 49% and killings have doubled since restrictions on public life were introduced (5/01/2020). When the lockdown was first implemented however, hotline calls rose 65% (BBC 3/03/2020).

In the States, in Vinton County, Ohio, things were already in crisis mode. This county has the lowest population in Ohio with the highest incidence of drug addiction, and this has already had a devastating impact on children. "Now, with social distancing measures in place in Vinton County and schools and churches closed, teachers and clergy, those who are the likeliest to come in contact with abused children, aren't, so they can't report cases of abuse." Kimes-Brown, a lawyer in Vinton, says that she suspects that is what is behind recent reductions in child abuse reports nationwide. "We've lost all those connections with our kids," she says (NPR, 4/29/2020). But the reduction in child abuse reporting is not true everywhere. Neighbors, friends, mail carriers, anyone who hears anything, who knows anything, who suspects anything is being encouraged to report what they see or hear. Kimes-Brown continues, "I don't think people realize how much information one report can provide," she says. "There are so many cases that I could say have been decided or made because an eyewitness came across the tiniest bit of information and reported it" (NPR). All of the normal places where people would go to get help, AA, NA, churches, and face-to-face therapy, have not been available. For obvious reasons, telehealth therapy is hardly helpful and certainly not confidential in these situations.

I think most are aware that women face abuse and murder everywhere, but the statistics in Mexico are always shocking. Even so, there has been a rise in those cases. The current report from February to April is that 1000 women have been murdered (The Independent, April 28, 2020). No more about the statistics needs to be laid out here. Suffice it to say, being home alone with abusers, with children who need supervision, without money, without a job, and getting low on food, has created a perfect storm where pre-existing, frightening situations are escalating.

You do not need to know more about what keeps me awake. You are reading this little volume because it promises help and solutions. There are ways you can reach out for help and ways to create some safety. Two therapists, Shari Schnuelle and Melissa Adams, were asked to contribute their expertise and provide help. Ms. Schnuelle's area of work, training, and experience is in trauma. She explains how this time of the virus has triggered people and raised anxiety levels. Then she gives practical steps for dealing with it. Ms. Adam's chapter is focused on her area of expertise, domestic abuse. She provides a scenario that is probably common to couples under the current stress of the stay-at-home orders. Then, of course, she provides ways to try to de-escalate tension, anger, and even danger, and keep the family safe.

I am fortunate. I live alone with my little service animal. We are safe and content. I cannot do much at this time to help, but I can create a vehicle for help to get to you. My hope is that as you read, you'll be encouraged, helped, and given some hope. Stay strong!

You, Me, Staying At Home

Shari Schnuelle, LIMHP, LPC

What is it like to be a mental health professional in a stay-at-home order for months? Probably a lot like your situation, except that I have a foot in two worlds, one where I am a person folks come to for answers and one where I notice my own responses, wondering, "Is this real? Am I overreacting? Underreacting? Where is the guidebook for this scenario, anyway?" Yes, there are people who, for political or other reasons, have chosen to believe the virus is all a giant plot, or is unreal, or not a risk. They aren't going to be buying this book; it's not for them. This booklet is for those of us who are living, perhaps white-knuckled, perhaps from a position of privilege, through something that hasn't been experienced quite this way before now. Also, these few paragraphs don't even try to take a deep dive into the difficulties essential workers are facing, or single-parents, those without helpful friends or relatives nearby. It is also limited to observations from my tiny slice of experience with Covid-19 where I live. Still, my hope is that it may be helpful in some way.

As a person with the usual assortment of friends, colleagues, family, and a small private practice, my life involves planning for the future and executing those plans, sometimes solo and other times in partnership with my husband. I look ahead, considering what my clients might need when I consider treatment planning and what is happening in the world, in our little metro area, and how it may affect their lives. Like you, my life also involves being flexible and changing to plan B, or M, or Z, as information/needs change and as the situation demands. From home management, taking care of kids, thinking about my own workload and what needs done for my clientele, life really does change day to day—but not like this. Not this big. Not with this scope.

I routinely mine my own life and my friends' lives for comparative experiences. I've learned to observe my own responses in real-time and then deliberately capture that information to try to use it to help my clients, because if I'm thinking it, feeling it or dealing with it, they surely are, too. That's an important lesson, right there—we are much more alike than we are different. So, as I bought gloves and a refillable jug of hand sanitizer and started laying in a few extra supplies—things I routinely bought that we would use no matter what—looking ahead to what the future might hold, I constantly asked myself, am I being realistic? Am I being a freak? Is this overreaction?

Staying Safe While Sheltering in Place

Am I panic-buying? What do we *need* and what is a fear-based purchase? (Put those *back*!) There's a bit of a dual nature in being a mental health practitioner, and I'm very aware of it through this unwanted, unlooked-for journey into Covid-19-world because I'm scared too—for my family, friends, clients, community, country, people I care about overseas, and my own health. I use the duality to help people come to see that their fears are not irrational, that they can be broken down into smaller bits and conquered, or at least managed, and that we're going through similar things. This is a skill I try to teach every client if they don't already have the ability, and it especially applies when one is in an unprecedented, world-wide pandemic: Think and plan ahead, do what you can, focus on the good—you've prepared for the not-good as much as you are able.

From Denial To Reality:

Trying to make sense of what is happening at breakneck speed, I look over notes I've made now that we're past the beginning stage of this beast. There are some common clusters of questions clients have asked. There are initial reality-testing questions they ask to check in and validate their concerns because they worry they are overreacting. Previously traumatized clients have to contend with traumatic retriggering and ask about their strong feelings of déjà-vu. Most everyone asks practical questions about how to manage activities of daily life, and as time goes on, concerns arise about the changes we are living through lingering for a very long time. So, we have an initial anxious response, we start to adjust, then we begin to adapt in earnest. Finally, as time grinds on, I'm hearing about quarantine-fatigue and observing peoples' vision shifting forward to a different type of future.

A teen I see, who has an inordinate love of dystopian fiction, said to me, with some satisfaction, "See? It's happening. I knew it would. I knew I didn't have to plan for college...the world is falling apart." Grace's apparent happiness at a seemingly self-fulfilling prophecy led me to ask, "So have you already prepared for this?" At that moment, Grace's face registered the realization that nothing was prepared; as a high school student, she was entirely unready and still dependent on her family. I could see her flip into "OMG" mode. This was the first moment that Grace realized, on an intimate and highly personal level, that the Covid crisis *would* affect her life. She started thinking about everything that might change in the world at large and in her personal experience, and it scared her. Reasonably so. Her earlier protests of not wanting to go to college—because that would be knuckling down to her parents' expectations—vaporized when she realized she might not even have the option. As classes moved to online, prom was cancelled and graduation left up in the air, Grace said, "This isn't happening." She shook her head like she was dreaming.

Grace is not alone in expecting disaster in my tiny slice of the clinical pie, in a small midwestern city. However, the bulk of my clients first came in with questions about their own stability—experiencing the very early coverage they saw in media (if they saw any at all), had led them to feel that they were safe. The disconnect was disconcerting. "This is a problem overseas and we are so far away, surely it can't affect us?" Questioning your own perspective is a normative response for a species that lives in groups. We *have to* get along. It's part of the social contract. It is to the overall benefit of the larger group if we are mostly all on the same page, so we check in with each other. Even in America, land of rugged individualism and self-determination as we like to tell ourselves, we compare ourselves with our peers, neighbors, families, friends, and coworkers. That is perhaps the largest function of social media—finding out "What is everyone else up to?" It makes some sense to consider that you yourself might be off a little bit, rather than figuring you're right and everyone else is wrong. We are taught, even in a society that highly prizes individualism, not to stick out too much, especially at certain life stages, such as Grace in high school. So, if most everyone else seems to be acting the way they usually do, we may go along much as we have, but if people are panicking and buying three years' worth of toilet paper, then perhaps we should do that, too?

Besides our neighbors, friends, family, coworkers, and social media influencers, we look to our leaders, to public figures and those charged with our welfare to see how they are behaving. Are they alarmed? Are they downplaying the crisis? Throughout February I heard growing choruses of, "Am I crazy to be worried about this? Government doesn't seem worried," with a descant of "It will never come *here.*" Toward the end of the month, the new verse was, "Is this *really* serious?" I heard people asserting that if they got Covid-19, it wouldn't be that bad. "It's just a flu!" I also heard people soothing themselves that the bad thing wouldn't touch them. There was, and continues to be, some comfort in denial, even thinking they probably already had it and didn't know it yet. None of this would keep coming up so repeatedly if people were not aware of and worried by the possibilities on some level, though. The sense of anxiety became widespread and pervasive. In session, we talked about "existential dread" daily.

As people became more tuned in to national news, especially what was happening overseas and on our coasts, that feeling of dread grew. As infections spread from country to country and cases grew world-wide, I started hearing in session, "This all feels so unreal. Why isn't anyone doing anything?" When Italy's struggles became nightly news, the overseas issue became more real, and as cases started piling up in New York City and the West coast, people I interacted with began to see it as a slow-motion crisis. Even though disease and death were happening to other people in other states, counties, and towns, it was somewhat removed...until it was in *our* state, our county, our town, and then it got real. Within about a month to six weeks' time, as soon as someone they knew became ill, the world turned upside down.

Staying Safe While Sheltering in Place

Throughout March, attention to news sources and media grew and even became compulsive. Many people fixated on news sources, almost obsessively reading everything they could get in their hands or on their browsers, anxiously and sometimes for hours and hours per day. Scouring multiple news sources was reassuring and gave a sense of control, but with the news changing hour by hour, including medical advice that changed rapidly, it produced a dopamine hit when someone found a new tidbit of information. That momentary reward reinforced the urge to just sit on the internet all day long for those who could. A number of people I saw put off sleep, chores, activities of daily living, like showering or laundry, whenever possible because it just felt *better* somehow to be on-line, reading about the disease, searching for some-thing new. Reading about symptoms was a push/pull of reassurance (I don't have it) and fear (maybe I do). We looked at what the others in our groups did, reading, watching and listening intently to add to our own knowledge so we could decide what *we* would do, for ourselves or loved ones, and whether it was a real problem or not. The intense focus produced two reactions, in that some people felt competent and prepared, whereas others became overwhelmed and even shut down.

The human mind typically favors action—for so many people, it feels better to make a decision rather than to be in the process of deciding. We can use that bias to help deal with anxieties and future concerns. It's not that a person can't or should not worry; that seems to be built-in to our psyches. What I encourage is to operationalize: make those worries functional instead of paralyzing. Worrying can be reframed as thinking ahead. Making lists of concerns, then organizing and preparing to take reasonable action can help people calm their fears. Having a plan can help people decrease free-floating anxiety and feel some sense that there is a bit of control, even if it's very, very small. Weird action might feel better, yet not really be that helpful. Some who hoarded toilet paper felt better, even if they didn't have enough food stocked up at home, so it is still important to try to have a broad perspective on which actions are most useful, and not act solely out of anxiety.

Déjà Vu: Trauma Response

As a trauma survivor and a person with PTSD (in remission), I personally have a feeling of déjà vu because, while I've not been involved to this extent in a worldwide pandemic in the past, (H1N1 brushed by us where I live), I do recognize the feeling of "What, THIS? *AGAIN*?" It's a common feeling for survivors of past trauma, as our overly sensitized, PTSD-influenced limbic systems send fight-flight-freeze-WHAT-theHELL messages to the brain. This isn't about being in the exact same circumstances repeatedly, it's about being in a situation in which one is not in control, where responses are limited, or perhaps where there is no real escape, so we are forced to find a way to get through it. Some people with PTSD will function better in a crisis situation than they do in everyday life because crisis itself is so familiar and has been neurologically normalized as their lived experience. This may also depend on whether you've dealt with your original trauma and how long ago your most recent traumatic experience was. For many people who have been traumatized in the past, the message of danger will feel uncomfortably familiar, even though the 'enemy' is invisible this time, a tiny virus that can change the lives of every person on the planet. The situation is different, but the physical and emotional responses may be exactly the same.

While trauma responses are as individual as the people who survive it, one type of trauma survivors are always on alert; they constantly scan for trouble. These are the people looking at the far horizons and keeping a keen eye out for danger; their limbic systems don't quiet all the way down and they are usually on alert, at least a little bit, even in everyday life situations. These people tend toward anxiety and will often have a "do SOMETHING" response, even if the things they do aren't completely useful. This is a common way "flee" manifests in adults and teens and could explain a portion of the hoarding/buying behavior we saw early on, although clearly some people were just profiteering.

A portion of traumatized people may freeze so no forward progress can be made. Their limbic system responses are so strong they shut down to try to survive. It's an adaptive response if you are a little bunny in the grass trying to evade the eye of the hawk, but not so much when there is limited time to respond adequately to a health crisis like Covid-19. This freeze response is not under a person's conscious control, there is no blame to lay. It is an added layer of difficulty for previously harmed people already in a difficult situation. If you find yourself freezing, ask for help. Reach out. Even just telling a friend, "I'm stuck, I don't know what to do first," could help you become unstuck.

There are traumatized people who have an angry response. They're over it. They've been hurt in the past and they're tired of having to deal with crises, put out fires, or survive some horrible situation. They're mad. They say, "Not AGAIN!" No, it doesn't mean that they had already lived through a quarantine-level international pandemic, rather that these particular people who have PTSD or have been previously harmed have a deep-level, leftover belief that other 'bad things' will come to them, that those bad things are inevitable, and they're sick of it. They may not know the particulars but do know that the bad thing, which is looming, unspecified, lurking out there in the darkness, *will* come and get them at some point. So, while they aren't surprised that something horrible is happening, they recognize it with incredulity, déjà vu, and frequently, anger. Yet anger is not necessarily a bad thing. It has energy and can make forward motion happen. In some ways, anger is more functional than the frozen response. Anger can propel a person to action and to set a boundary: Not here. Not now. Not me. Setting a boundary against an existential threat can be as simple as the resilience mindset that, no matter what happens, I will be fine. I *will* find a way.

But What Do I Do?:

When the Covid situation began feeling real to people, clients started thinking about what is going to happen here, to us, in this town/city/state? The crisis has become more clearly defined and it has become obvious that "normal life" has departed, at least for now. Questions about how to access resources were a huge part of the beginning of March. Concerns about how to keep ourselves physically safe and healthy also came to the fore. For example, what should I do if I accidentally touch my face? What can substitute for disinfecting wipes now that they're impossible to find? Individuals and families alike had to figure out how to keep themselves fed, pay bills, and access resources to deal with the crisis at a time when shortages were apparent and the disease was spreading mostly silently. Some had to decide whether to go home to help parents and shelter safely with them, or to remain sheltered in place.

That early scramble just to make sure there was enough food, medicine, supplies, and cleaning materials occupied every waking minute, even as people were still working in their jobs before stay-at-home orders were set. People learned new routines of how to clean, how to wear gloves or wash hands more thoroughly, how to wear masks, and how to avoid cross-contamination. Sleep was shattered, undermining immune systems precisely when we needed to be at our healthiest to fight off the illness. Add to this the fact that nobody seemed to know how long this health crisis would last, or even how long shelter-in-place would last. The idea of 18-24 months for a vaccine bred hopelessness among some clients. It is very difficult to plan ahead and try to imagine what a person or family will need for the next two years—it was paralyzing for more than one person. More recent news that an 18-24 month timeline is likely unrealistic has definitely aggravated fears.

Parents of younger children face an especially difficult situation in that their children are often too young to be able to follow safety recommendations, touching their faces, putting everything in their mouths, hugging their friends, hanging out in far too close proximity. Parents deemed essential workers still had access to daycare, but there was a lot more fear about dropping the kids off on the way to work. Many healthcare workers sequestered themselves from their families to keep others safe, but plenty of single parents could not do this. I heard that more than one parent sadly gave their child over to a relative to take care of for safety because their own schedule and exposures were so uncertain.

Dixie texted me urgently asking if she could have an emergency online session, *right now.* She was crying and said her friend told her to call; she'd been trying to hold it back but had instead been "leaking" tears in dribbles and drabs for three days. Dixie asked, "How do I keep my sanity? It's unrelenting! I am working more now at home than I did when I went to work in my office, and there's no escape!" Dixie was trying to work, teach, run the home, and manage all the normal work of getting groceries with new standards for contact, exposure, sanitization, and cleanliness that are much more extreme than usual. She was sleeping less because of the current crisis, but also due to being exhausted to the point that her sleep was broken and she was wakeful, not getting the deeper healing sleep her body and mind really needed.

Added to her own problems, her kids were not sleeping, eating, or behaving as well as they used to because their routines had been entirely upended as well, and they could see the tension in Mom. They feel that something was wrong. They didn't understand what was happening but sensed change that they didn't like, and they were scared. This wasn't just an early summer vacation because they were still going to school online; Mom was home now all the time, yet they couldn't have friends over. They couldn't go to friends' houses or even visit family as they normally would. Something was different and it felt bad.

Children are suffering, too. For people who have a partner to share the load, it's still a struggle, and Dixie doesn't have a partner in the home. Dealing with it all feels overwhelming. Parents often make shortcuts in their own wellness and self-care, prioritizing their family's needs over their own, just trying to get by.

Holes in our social safety net showed up very quickly, even for people who thought they were well covered or had resources lined up. This isn't the place for political discourse; it suffices to say that, of the people I work with, around 80% became aware of glaring problems with supporting their families, providing for physical safety, staying healthy, and managing children. Vital workers had to find a safe place for their children. For those who could work from home, a new problem arose—what to do with kids who were supposed to be doing online school at the same time the parent was supposed to be working? How can one be a teacher, employee and parent simultaneously? Preschool children need a lot of watching, which can make working from home seem impossible. Asking for help is the right thing to do. It is especially hard for single parents or people whose partners work in a field where they may be absent for an extended time, such as healthcare frontline providers and essential employees. People without a strong social network face real problems in trying to manage their young family members.

Coping, Seriously

As soon as practicalities were largely handled and as time stretched out, the themes that came up repeatedly boiled down to, "How do I not lose my mind?"

Keeping one's sanity lies in realizing this is an abnormal situation. In unprecedented circumstances, it is actually normal not to know what the hell is going on. We don't live through world-wide novel virus pandemics often, and aren't we all so thankful for that? In an abnormal situation, the usual routines will probably not work. We have to do something new. Adapting to what is happening right now, instead of trying to impose the old 'normal,' will probably work better. Get relentlessly practical and find a new normal: here is what we can do today. Now we go to school online. Now we order groceries if we can and wipe off certain things before bringing them in the home. Now we work from home. Now we wash our hands a lot longer than we may have before. We redefine normal; normal is whatever we are doing *now*.

Now we stay apart from people we normally would hug and cuddle, to keep them safe and ourselves healthy. Online contact is better than nothing, but it can physically hurt to not touch your loved ones, not be able to go visit them, not see new or beloved faces in person, face to face. People can become skin-hungry, where they just really need physical touch. For those living alone, this is a serious problem. Asking for what you need is the solution, so if you are not alone, ask for hugs. Ask for back scratches. Cuddle if you can—people, pets, stuffed animals, whatever you have available. For those alone, or for whom it would not be appropriate to ask, some self-soothing techniques, such as rocking, brushing hair, putting on lotion, even just massaging your own feet & hands, can be helpful in a pinch.

Frankly, unless you are unusually privileged and have loads of help, just *let your standards drop already*. I don't mean to fling everything you value to the wind, but you likely won't be able to maintain all that was regular and routine with your pre-virus life. I suggest, quite strongly, that you thoughtfully choose a few actions, routines, ideals or habits that matter the very most to you. What is part of your identity, and what is just the way you *want* to live? Focus on the most important, and *let the rest go.*

If your daily laundry becomes once a week, that saves you some hassle. If reading is important to you but you find you can't concentrate, maybe you can try an audiobook to see if that works better? If you make perfectly planned, nutritionally balanced meals and it stresses you, loosen up... but if planning those meals gives you comfort and it's something you find meaningful, do your best with what you have to work with, knowing you will also face the reality of pandemic-world: we are not in control. Things you like to eat or feed your family might be unavailable, so Plan B. Or Plan M. Or even Plan Z. Are people eating? Are tummies full? Look at the bigger picture: You're alive. Maybe even blessed. Let. It. Go. Several people I work with chucked their old routine entirely, giving 'pandemic life' a lick and a prayer—they let go of a LOT... and found out that some things they thought were absolutely crucial really were not anymore. Life at home in quarantine has been eye-opening as far as what is a want and what is a need.

It's great if you can set up some kind of structure, and it doesn't need to be huge. I encourage folks to make a small schedule because a big one is likely going to become a source of frustration. We don't have control; we don't know what we're doing. Information is coming at us and changing, literally, by the hour or minute. This is fly-by-the-seat-of-your-pants territory. Trust yourself. Believe in your own ability to make good decisions. You can still sort out what is a good choice and what is not, but if you're really wavering, reality-test it with your partner, your friends, online sources, and with whomever you can communicate. Perhaps it doesn't work for you to still wake at 6, drag kids out of bed, and have your old, clock-driven routines based on office commutes and school schedules. Find out what happens if the kids go to bed later but also get up later, and you get some blessed time alone with your own thoughts after they've gone to bed. People who cling rigidly to one idea of *The Way That Things Must Be* are going to fare poorly in a world that thinks it's entirely okay to throw mutant new viruses at all of us. Modified free-range parenting, with common-sense limits, might just save you some gray hairs and be the way through while we all adapt to whatever it is we are doing now (the new abnormal).

Here are some basics that you can adapt to your own living situation:

- Exercise—try to get some. It's generally good for you and helps you be healthy, but most of all, it burns off anxious energy. Even an ambling walk is good. You don't have to set land-speed records.

- Get some sunlight on your forehead. It lifts your mood, your body will make some needed Vitamin D, and so many people report feeling better once they've had a bit of sun.

- Eat well—as well as you can, knowing that this is an area you'll have to be flexible on as shortages and supply chains adapt to the crisis.

- Prioritize sleep; sleep as well as you can and keep trying to improve it. Consult with your doctor if you are not sleeping restfully, as poor sleep can hurt your immune response and leave you more vulnerable to illness. Poor sleep can also add to mental health struggles; our bodies need sleep to be as stable as possible. Sleep hygiene suggestions are all over the internet, but one of the simplest is to keep the place you sleep cool and dark.

- Create small rituals—find something you really enjoy, even if it feels cheesy, then stick to it. The people banging pots and pans at 7 p.m. each night in support of healthcare workers? It's wonderful. It's an outlet. That's a small ritual. In Colorado, they're howling into the sky each night around 7 and you can hear the cry taken up block to block in Denver—that's a ritual. Find something and regularly, fiercely, do it.

- Actively search for delight—small beauties, something that speaks to your lovely little soul; find it, grab it and hold it tight. I've taken delight in the new baby bunnies bouncing around drunkenly in the backyard. I'm noticing the teeny purple flowers growing in the flowerbed where they don't belong but have assertively pushed their way in; they're probably invasive. I don't care, they're lovely. They belong now. Whatever it is that catches your notice, pay attention. Notice deeply. See if it fills something in you that was longing to be filled…and if so? Cling to it.

- Grab some humor, even dark humor. We feel better with belly laughs. It can seem incongruous to laugh hard during a very tough time in the world, but it is a light in a dark tunnel and you'll notice your mood and optimism rebound almost instantly. Whether it's watching old movies, falling down weird YouTube rabbit-holes or just meme-hunting online, find *your* thing to laugh at and then do it like it's medicine, because it is. Laughing in the dark is an act of bravery.

- Learn from others' mistakes—friends or strangers, IRL, or online. Remember to wear pants when you Zoom. Put clothing on whenever someone has a laptop around. Try not to streak through your partner's online work meeting, much less your own. If you want to be able to meet your coworkers' eyes ever again, do not take your phone with you into the bathroom, especially not if you are in a meeting.

- Get dirty. Garden, plant flowers, or care for a single succulent if that's all you can keep alive. Hands in soil mellow the angsty soul. Get into nature any way you can. If you're lucky enough to have a yard or some dirt you can dig into and fiddle with, do it!

- Be brave. Try something new like learning a language if that's even a remote possibility for you in this situation. Search for "how to" do something you've always wanted to try, for example, "How to sing like a Broadway singer." Learning something new challenges your brain and causes new neuronal growth. If that's too much, maybe there's a skill, craft, or hobby you've always wanted to try or get back to. Learn one of those Tik-Tok dances. Paint pouring is messy fun with no pressure on the outcome. Finger-paint with your kids. Scribble while you take notes. Doodle mindlessly and then turn the doodle around and see what it looks like. Sing outside and see what your neighbors think. Howl into the night sky.

- Serve others—even if you need help, yourself. If you can be of help to someone else in any way, it not only helps them but has a wonderful effect in lifting your own spirits. If you can, donate time, donate cash, donate materials, or donate food. Do something for a locked-in neighbor. Sew masks. Look at your community and see if there is any way you can be of service. It also helps in case you yourself ever need assistance. If you know you have given of your own free will, when it's your turn to ask for help, you can accept it knowing it was given with an open and cheerful heart.

Break It Down

I say this often enough that my clients want to hurt me, "How do you eat an elephant? One bite at a time." (Please don't eat elephants, it's a metaphor.)

Staying Safe While Sheltering in Place

Break overwhelming issues down into manageable bits. Even something as old-fashioned as making a list and then tackling one single item can work. One of my clients has a master list and then a daily list—it works for him! Taking teeny tiny steps will still get you where you need to go eventually and can create the momentum that empowers you to take bigger steps when you feel ready. That's also why I suggest making a small schedule for structure, so you can easily pivot and see what *works*. Throw out whatever doesn't...revise, refine your results, and you'll get to something that works just right for you. That's the part that really matters. When the weight of existential dread is pressing down on you, that is the time to be gentle with yourself and do the least, smallest, most meaningful step you can that starts you on your way. Progress is much more important than perfection.

It's also good to get comfortable with ambiguity. In this weird world that we find ourselves in, most folks don't know what they're doing. Here's the secret: <u>We don't always have to.</u> Healthcare workers, support, and essential workers are all trying to save lives and keep our way of living intact, yet we all put one foot in front of the other to weather this crisis in our different ways. Nobody knows what our world is going to look like when this is "over with," or even what that means, or when. However you get there is probably fine. Focusing on what is in front of us is manageable. You don't have to know all the answers, and it's okay to tell kids, friends, parents, or coworkers, "I don't know. Yet." Three months ago, or six, or a year ago, could you have imagined what life would look like right now? Just three months ago, I was finalizing details for a high school graduation party that will most likely not happen. It's sad he won't get to go through those ceremonies, and yet what a privilege it is to miss them instead of missing a family member lost to Covid-19. Find a substitute. We can't see the future. Plan M. Plan Z.

Fear Spirals Are Dreadful

The feeling of existential dread that we're all living with can easily grow into fear spirals, and they're not helpful to anyone. A fear spiral is catastrophizing, awfulizing, thinking only of the most horrible outcome, and dwelling on that. They can lead to panic attacks and freezing. With the whole world feeling uneasy, anxiety is contagious. Doing what you can to control your mind and stop the escalation is important for your wellness and for those around you. That can involve a spiritual practice, meditation or prayer, or a contemplative practice as you define it. Knitting is mindfulness in action! There are other psychological techniques like thought substitution or getting completely sideways and using creativity to change your neurological state. Some folks sing, some paint, others dance—whatever you can do to stop the awfulizing—it's important to do that. Don't let your mind run away with itself.

- DBT (dialectical behavioral therapy) is a form of therapy that helps people be in the moment and not let their feelings run the show. There are abundant free resources online that are worth looking into. Telehealth is widely available now, but if you can't afford or access it, even working through the worksheets online might help.

• Authors like Byron Katie, https://thework.com/, teach how to turn locked-in ideas upside down and escape the fear spiral. Eckhardt Tolle's *The Power of Now* is compelling. Audiobooks can work if you find you don't have the ability to focus and read right now. There are a multitude of bloggers and vloggers and Ted Talks to change your mindset. Even inspirational, aspirational sites like Pinterest can change your perspective.

• Distract your thoughts by using your senses— that can work beautifully. A sensory kit can just be a baggie full of things that get your attention—something you can smell, see, hear, touch, feel. Find a pungent smell, a strong taste, a beautiful picture, a soothing touch, music, or a rhythm that moves your body and stirs your heart—and *use* those things. It's worth finding out what works for you. You'll want to gather these items ahead of time because when you are overwhelmed, you won't be able to think well. Prepare and have it easily accessible so you can just grab it if you're in an awful spot. Mind is what the brain does: IF you earnestly employ these distractions, you'll activate different parts of your brain, which can change what you're thinking and feeling. This is a tried-and-true technique for dealing with flashbacks, but it can be used for distressing situations of all sorts.

- Physical movement, even just walking around your apartment or home, or outdoors if you can do that, can realign your whole thought process. The discipline is to do something about it when you find yourself caught up in fear. Don't just sit there in it. Yoga is exceptional at helping people grow strong, center themselves, and learn to tolerate distress, and there are free sources online for even the most physically challenged people. Change your body, change your mind, do something different.

Who Knows What Comes Next

Some of what comes next can be guessed at. The disruption of the past few months may lead to risk-taking behavior as some people break out of restrictions. We will probably see new virus outbreaks and hotspots happening in waves. It could be a long time until there is a vaccine or reliable treatment available. Preexisting mental health issues may worsen and new ones arise, not only because of death but even due to social changes like not being able to congregate the way we're used to. We're social animals, and something as simple as going to the movies may disappear for a while; we just don't have the same shared experience while all streaming at the same time in our individual homes. Group activities are going to look very different or disappear for some time. Naturally, we look to healthcare providers risking their lives, getting sick, having to witness so much death, and being forced to do it without proper PPE precautions, but even among people who are not front-line there will likely be an uptick in mental health and other PTSD diagnoses due to the disruption we're living through. There has been so much loss already, but much we can't even guess at: what will summer be like without parks and swimming pools being open? How about kids who are used to participating in athletic teams, special interest camps, sleep-away camps, and running around with friends? Professional sports, concerts, fairs? There are things we have always taken for granted and we can't even guess how Covid-19 will affect them.

The tyranny of low-wage jobs has come to the forefront. People we rely on right at this very moment are suffering and *wish* they could stay home. Frequently, those who provide essential services, like grocery workers and delivery persons, are paid poorly. That should probably change. There are people who are risking their lives for us, not only healthcare workers who are going above and beyond at peril to their own health, but also those who go to work in a place that is difficult to make safe—like meatpacking plants, or factories that make essential goods. Do they have to face that horrible choice? To pay bills and put food on the table, workers risk their own health and the danger of carrying the virus back to family members, because they can't not work. Can we not find a better way with a functional social safety net?

So, if we grieve for people lost, for norms that have changed, and for the parts of life that we liked fine and didn't want to change, it might be good to also wonder about that old way of living. We're adapting all the time to the way things are now, whether we like it or not. Can we also notice if parts of *now* are actually better than *before*? Some are clearly much, much worse, but it might be that some of the ways we used to live *needed* to adapt and change. We're now recognizing how interconnected we all are. Many people I work with remark that they are spending much less and feel better for it. There are a number of articles online about slower pleasures, and we're learning about unnecessary busyness. Some people were busy as a point of pride, buzzing through their lives in a haze of activity that surely seemed essential. I know someone who struggled to stay home just one day a week, but when the virus forced her to stay in, she realized it was calming, grounding. Not so bad.

Our world is not going to look the same as it used to. I don't know if it will ever go back to the old "normal," although I suppose it might. Even watching TV or movies feels odd right now when we see scenes of people close to one another, huddled together, with all the careless, casual touch. It won't be surprising if people are standoffish or afraid of germ transmission in our "after." The questions are really not when will we get back to 'normal,' but should we, and what will that look like? Think about those things that you long for right now—did you know they meant so much to you? Were you aware of what you took for granted? Those are the things that need to be prioritized as we define our new normal and as we begin the process of re-establishing not only our economy but our society.

We are experiencing "quarantine fatigue." Folks are quite sick of being indoors, not socializing, not living their regular lives. We like to hang out together, and our interconnections contribute to health and wellness. Social bonds have been stretched so painfully during this time. We can use this information to strengthen our connections and improve areas that have glaringly come to light as unfair, biased, and unequal. This time we've lived through can be put to use as a wake-up call to improve our world, rather than something we merely endured and brushed off as quickly as possible. If we forget the lessons about preparedness, about treasuring our bonds with others, about caring for our wellness and wholeness as a society, the lessons of this pandemic will have been wasted. We're better than that. Let's not waste our opportunity to reshape the world into something that fits and works better for people at all levels of society.

A Case in Point:
Pam and Steve

Melissa Adams, LICSW, CDC

Pam lives with her husband, Steve, and their two grade-school children. There have been fights in the past where Steve has pushed Pam, slapped her, pulled her hair, and even choked her. Pam considered leaving many times, but she decided to wait until the kids were older before trying to leave and file for divorce. She feared that if the kids were very little when she left, Steve might neglect or even hurt them during his parenting time, and they wouldn't be old enough to come home and tell her what had happened. Before the Covid-19 emergency happened, Pam had saved enough money to talk to an attorney and she had a plan. She told her attorney that when she was ready to leave, she would call and ask that papers be filed and that Steve be served with papers at work, so she would have time to get the locks changed on the house and the attorney could get an emergency order for her to have full custody and for Steve to be excluded from the house for the duration of the divorce proceedings. But when the national emergency happened and Steve was furloughed from his job as a cook at a local restaurant, Pam and the kids were stuck in the house all day, nearly every day, with Steve. He has become much more volatile now that he is worried about their finances and cannot go to the dart leagues that he enjoys on Tuesday and Thursday nights. Pam has done her best to keep the kids on track with their at-home schooling, while still working some drive-up shifts at the bank where she is a part-time teller. Steve has assaulted her twice since the stay-home order was issued in their state, and she doesn't know when she will be able to get in touch with her attorney, or how she will get Steve served with papers when he is always home. Pam feels trapped and hopeless at times. Right now, Pam's best times are when she is tucking her kids in at night, or when she works a Saturday morning at the bank, when Steve is probably still asleep and the kids are quietly watching tv.

Pam's reality is something that many people are facing as the pandemic continues to rage through our communities. Maybe you or someone you know is sitting in a situation like Pam's right now. Please know that there are still things you can do to stay safe at home and ways you can reach out for help when you need it.

Two especially important factors to keep in mind when there has been violence in a relationship and there is a potential for it to happen again:

Staying Safe While Sheltering in Place

1) You need to do or say whatever you have to, in order to placate the abusive partner and keep them from escalating.

2) Safety overrules accountability. This means that when you are in a potentially dangerous situation, it is better to be safe than to call someone out on their abusive behaviors or statements, which may just escalate things further.

While there are many situations that contribute to family violence, parenting and money matters are two of the most common.

Difficulty With Kids

Kids are on edge and struggling right now, sometimes not getting schoolwork done or arguing with parents and siblings. In this time of social distancing and perhaps even quarantine, kids cannot do some of the many things that they usually do to de-stress such as play at the park, go play at friends' houses, attend birthday parties and enjoy extended family. They may also be hearing adults speak of the pandemic or hear or watch news talking about deaths and other frightening topics. Do your best to help them get outside and play in the sunshine as much as possible, even if only on the front porch or in the backyard, because this will help to reduce arguments when they've been inside too long. Also recognize that when kids are trying to learn school subjects online without the usual help from a teacher, it can be overwhelming and frustrating, so they will sometimes simply refuse to try or refuse to finish an assignment. Do not take these behaviors personally or interpret them as being disrespectful toward you. Recognize that they don't have all the knowledge and experience you have in dealing with hard things and they need assistance and encouragement, not criticism and threats, to help them keep trying. It is helpful to give kids some predictability in their lives, such as set times to get up and go to bed, set meal and snack times, and set hours for schoolwork, breaks, outside time, and quiet play time.

Money And Financial Issues

Money concerns are a real fear for many right now, especially when money may be a major concern and one or both of you is laid off or working far fewer hours. It is important to balance between minimizing a problem and making it an enormous problem. You can't pretend that it isn't a concern if you don't have enough for rent this month, but it won't help to rage about how unfair all of this is and how other people don't have it as badly. Try discussing what help there might be available for certain money problems, in a united effort to solve the problem, instead of being angry with each other for not seeing it in the same light. Many utility companies are not shutting off service right now, even if payments are late or unpaid. Many landlords and mortgage companies are willing to offer deferment of payments, or arrangements for half payments, during this crisis. There are also stimulus monies that are coming out in the form of direct checks and increased amounts of unemployment compensation, as well as small business loans to keep paying payroll and health insurance for employees. Local agencies like United Way and food pantries, churches and other assistance agencies also have access to some emergency funds and can make referrals to other places for specific needs.

Try to avoid arguments about why you have certain payment obligations or debt right now. Going over why "we shouldn't have bought the vehicle or the house or the new furniture," will only make this worse. Those payments are due to choices made in the past, when you could not have anticipated this situation that would so drastically affect your income. Do the best you can to call creditors and make arrangements for half payments, deferred payments, or extended credit to help you manage for the next six months. Working together to make these calls can deflate a money argument.

Do your best to stay away from arguments about things you have spent money on in the past, such as cigarettes, alcohol, cable tv, extra tools, sporting events and hobbies. Simply agree that we will watch spending as best we can right now, while still keeping our family safe. If it makes sense to keep the cable tv or internet on, so that we all have something to distract us from our worries, keep the cable and the internet. Even though cigarettes are expensive, trying to stop smoking right now if you don't really want to will create more potential arguments. If you really want to try to cut down right now, go ahead, but don't make yourself and your family miserable to save a bit of money.

Essential Travel Outside The Home

Another potential argument area is where you will go, other than work. One of you might want to go to places that are still open, but the other may believe that is really an unnecessary outing. The person who thinks it is necessary is likely trying to get away from the feeling of being penned up and restricted, while the person who wants everyone to stay home is likely afraid they will contract the virus while out and about and potentially bring it home to the household. Many of us have varying differences in what we think is safe or dangerous behavior right now. Try talking about the fear or the frustration you are feeling at being stuck in the house. When you can each understand that you both might have a feeling other than anger, you are much more likely to come to a compromise or a way to make this situation safe enough for both of you to feel okay about a choice. The ultimate choice here is trying to prevent a physical altercation. It is understandable that you want to prevent the virus from coming into your home, but you can't let the argument progress to the point that a hospital visit for an injury will happen, either.

One very frightening situation is if an argument escalates to the point where one person says, "You have to get out now, and you cannot come back." Try to really assess if one person leaving is necessary for the safety of everyone in the house. If so, then a call to 911 is necessary, because police can help determine where someone should go if it is too dangerous for them to stay home. If the danger is not at that level, and you are both just really sick of each other, a strategy like two hours apart might help to deescalate the situation to the point where you can stand to be in the same house again. During a two hour "time away," it is good to avoid alcohol, and be responsible about saying when the person leaving will be home and, if possible, where they are going. One of you may want to "just drive around for a while" to cool off, which is fine, but it is only fair to stay in town, or in the neighborhood if your city is huge, so your partner won't be afraid, if you have been gone hours, that you have become sick or injured. Again, remember that safety is a priority over accountability. When the time away is over, returning to the argument to prove that you are right about something is a foolish endeavor. Simply drop the topic and agree that things will be better tomorrow. Come up with an activity to do that will help each of you feel comfortable and relaxed, such as watching a movie, going to bed early to read a book, playing a board game with the kids, or listening to some music that you both like.

Communication with People for Support or Help

There are many times when you need to just hear a supportive voice, telling you that you can do this hard thing and that you will be able to get out when the time is right. Texting is sometimes easier and safer than phone calls. Many shelters and domestic abuse hotlines now have numbers that can also accept text messages. If you get a chance to leave the house briefly by yourself, say for a trip to get a few necessary groceries, drive to a friend's house who you know is home and ask them to talk to you outside for a few minutes, or through the screen of their front door, to maintain physical distance. Make a plan with your friend that if you text or call them, you will use certain code words to let them know if you need them to come over and sit in the driveway in their car, or if they need to call police for you. If your friend can do so, ask them to get you a prepaid cell phone that you can pick up from them later or they can drop off to you. Keep the prepaid phone charged, but turned off, and hidden, but where you can get to it when you need it. A good place to hide something is in the bathroom in a box of feminine products, and a good place to charge it is in a seldom used room, plugged in behind a piece of furniture or a stack of folded blankets.

Safety During an Altercation

When you can tell that an incident is brewing and the abusive person appears to be escalating, there are a few things you can do to keep yourself as safe as possible if you can't leave the house. Stay in a room with soft furnishings, so if you are pushed against something, you are less likely to hit something hard. Bedrooms and living areas are better than kitchens and bathrooms. Try to avoid areas where you could get pushed into a closet or pushed down the stairs.

If the incident escalates such that you need to call 911, give your address first thing when you call, that way if the abuser smashed your phone, at least 911 got the address and will send a unit to you. If you can get out into the front yard of your home, then your neighbors are also more likely to see and hear what is happening and they will also call 911. More people are at home right now, and many are also working outside in their yards or out walking or riding bikes. The abuser is less likely to follow you out into the neighborhood if they can see people who will be witnesses to the event.

Plan In Case You Have To Leave And Get To Safety

While you are doing your best to keep things calm, there still may be an incident where you absolutely have to leave the house and may be gone for a while, either in an emergency shelter or with friends or relatives who can let you stay a while. Plan for that to be a possibility, so that you are ready to go quickly if it happens. Keep these items in a bag, hidden someplace where you can get to it on the way out the door: a few items of clothing, some for the kids if you are taking kids with you (especially underwear), a few days of any necessary prescriptions in a container (your pharmacy can get you emergency refills, but you will need a few days until they can do that), some cash, and an extra pair of shoes. If you have a spare key to your vehicle, put that in the bag also. Often, when someone needs to leave, the abuser has taken their keys and they don't have shoes on when it is time to go. If you need to leave your bag at your neighbor's house, in their unlocked garage or some other area that is easy to access, make those arrangements with your neighbor. You may be concerned about the safety of a shelter right now, with the need for social distancing. Many shelters have arrangements where they can put people in hotel rooms for the duration of an emergency, so they can still keep social distancing in place.

If You Have To Call Police And Your Partner Is Arrested:

If police are called to your home, do your best to talk to an officer out of the hearing range of your partner. Stress to police that your safety is seriously in jeopardy and that this is not an isolated incident. You can even ask that you and your kids be taken to a shelter if they are not going to arrest your partner. If your partner is arrested, keep in mind that there may be a bond hearing the very next morning, and you need to be in a safe place when that hearing happens. It is quite likely that your partner will bond out, given the concerns over keeping people incarcerated during a pandemic. Ask police for the phone number for the local domestic violence agency, where they can talk to you on the phone about possible shelter alternatives. You can also discuss with the agency how likely it is that a no contact order will be issued on your partner's bond, and how to keep yourself safe when there is a no contact order in place. Some agencies have funds to pay for emergency lock changes, and they can help you do safety planning on the phone, to plan for when your partner is released after the bond hearing.

Epilogue:
We Adapt, Survive and
Eventually, We Thrive:

Shari Schnuelle

Even in really awful circumstances, humans are adaptable creatures. We find a way to get through the unthinkable. None of us would be here if our ancestors had not figured out how to manage their own crises, from the dawn of time. In the case of intimate partner violence or abuse, we find methods of de-escalation, keeping ourselves and our children as safe as possible as we prepare to get away without harm. In the case of a worldwide pandemic, similarly we find ways to keep ourselves and those around us protected. In both situations, we find ourselves in a world that was unlooked-for and certainly unwanted. We change the way we do things to get to a better tomorrow. What carries us through is innate adaptability and belief in ourselves, predicated upon the possibility of a better future. As we navigate this crisis, complications will pop up individually and as a people, and we'll solve them. We'll heal them, fix them, and then face the inevitable new crises that arise. We'll work on those next. Whatever presents itself, we as a species don't give up, but keep hacking away at it until an acceptable resolution is found. Resilience is one of our greatest strengths.

Meet the Authors

Geri Henderson, PhD, is a professor for the University of Maryland Global Campus. She taught in a number of countries before moving to Germany, where she has lived with her service dog, Jami for the past 4 years. Geri enjoys teaching, research, writing, music, and reading. Her field of study was Interdisciplinary Medieval Studies, but she is also an experienced writing and literature teacher. Co-author, *Healing from Incest,* Collaborator, *Noah's New Puppy.*

Shari Schnuelle holds a BA in Psychology from the University of Nebraska-Lincoln and an M.S.Ed from the University of Nebraska-Kearney. She has over 20 years' experience offering traditional counseling, including depression and anxiety, with specialization in treating trauma, fostering trauma resilience, and post-traumatic growth. Shari also offers life coaching focused on creative growth, particularly for women in transition, who envision different directions in their lives. Shari can be reached at www.slscounseling.com and www.transformmylife.org. Her facebook pages are Shari L. Schnuelle PC Professional Counseling Services and Transform My Life.

Melissa Adams holds a degree in Psychology from Texas Christian University and a Master's of Social Work degree from the University of Nebraska. She received her formal life coach education from the Institute for Life Coach Training and Certified Divorce Coaching LLC.

Melissa's experience includes counseling for relationship difficulties, depression and anxiety, bipolar disorder, anger management, behavior disorders, family addiction patterns, and recovery from abuse. She has specialized her coaching services for divorcing families because families can navigate that major life change much more successfully when they have a "personal assistant" guiding them along the way. Melissa has over nineteen years of experience in working with families in different times of transition. Melissa can be reached at www.madamscounseling.com and www.daybreaklifecoach.com. Her facebook page is Life Coaching with Melissa Adams

MSI Press

Books in Our Pandemic Series

10 Quick Homework Tips (Alder & Trombly)

Choice and Structure for Children with Autism (McNeil)

Diary of an RVer during Quarantine (MacDonald)

Exercising in a Pandemic (Young)

God Speaks into Darkness (Easterling)

How to Stay Calm in Chaos: An Everyday Self-Care Guide (Gentile)

Learning Languages at Home (Leaver)

Old and On Hold (Cooper)

Porn and the Pandemic (Shea)

Seeking Balance in an Unbalanced Time (Greenebaum)

Staying Safe While Sheltering in Place (Schnuelle, Adams, & Henderson)

The Pandemic and Hope (Ortman)

Tips, Tools, and Anecdotes to Help with a Pandemic (Charnas)

CPSIA information can be obtained
at www.ICGtesting.com
Printed in the USA
BVHW042226141020
591099BV00007B/68